National Help Hotline

SAMHSA (MENTAL/SUBSTANCE) use disorders
1(800)662 - HELP (4357)

NATIONAL SUICIDE PREVENTION HOTLINE

1(800)273 - 8255

NATIONAL RUNAWAY SAFELINE

1(800)RUNAWAY

EVERY SOBER DAY IS A MIRACLE

Contact  Someone

Phone:
Address:

Phone:
Address:

Phone:
Address:

Phone:
Address:

Phone:
Address:

Phone:
Address:

Phone:
Address:

Phone:
Address:

EMERGENCY CONTACTS & ADDRESSES

Name:	Name:
Phone:	Phone:
Address:	Address:

EVERY SOBER DAY IS A MIRACLE

Contact  A Group

Phone:
Address:

Phone:
Address:

Phone:
Address:

Phone:
Address:

Phone:
Address:

Phone:
Address:

Phone:
Address:

Phone:
Address:

EMERGENCY CONTACTS & ADDRESSES

Name:	Name:
Phone:	Phone:
Address:	Address:

JANUARY

EVERY SOBER DAY IS A MIRACLE

Meeting Schedule

Date	Time	Group

EVERY SOBER DAY IS A MIRACLE

DATE: _____   DAYS SOBER: _____

QUOTE OF THE DAY

_____

_____

_____

_____

I FEEL . . .

HAPPY   >===================<   SAD
ENERGETIC >===================<   TIRED
CALM   >===================<   ANXIOUS

ANY URGES OR CRAVINGS?

YES   NO

COMMENTS:

EVERY SOBER DAY IS A MIRACLE

DATE: _____   DAYS SOBER: _____

QUOTE OF THE DAY

_____

_____

_____

_____

I FEEL . . .

HAPPY		SAD
ENERGETIC		TIRED
CALM		ANXIOUS

ANY URGES OR CRAVINGS?
_____ YES   _____ NO

COMMENTS: _____

DATE: DAYS SOBER:

QUOTE OF THE DAY

I FEEL . . .

HAPPY		SAD
ENERGETIC		TIRED
CALM		ANXIOUS

ANY URGES OR CRAVINGS?
YES   NO

COMMENTS:

EVERY SOBER DAY IS A MIRACLE

DATE: _____   DAYS SOBER: _____

QUOTE OF THE DAY

_____

_____

_____

_____

I FEEL . . .

HAPPY	⟨_____⟩	SAD
ENERGETIC	⟨_____⟩	TIRED
CALM	⟨_____⟩	ANXIOUS

ANY URGES OR CRAVINGS?
_____ YES   _____ NO

COMMENTS: _____

Date:

EVERY SOBER DAY IS A MIRACLE

Goals

MileStones

Why Am I Doing This?

What Are Your Struggles?

What Do You Struggle With The Most?
What Support Do You Need?

_____

_____

_____

What Is One Step You Can Take To
Work On Your Struggles?

_____

_____

_____

What Do You Need To Stay Sober?

_____

_____

_____

Prevention

Signs You're Struggling or Becoming Overwhelmed?

_____

_____

_____

Coping Skills To Use:

_____

_____

_____

What Gets You Back On Track?

_____

_____

_____

What Do You Love About Sobriety?

_____

_____

_____

REVIEW

How Has Your Addiction Affected Your Life?

What's The Worst Part About Your Addiction?

What Things Have You Learned From Your Struggles?

REVIEW

What Keeps Drawing You Back Into Your Addiction?

_____

_____

_____

How Have You Sabotaged Your Recovery In The Past?

_____

_____

_____

What Does Your Rock Bottom Look Like?

_____

_____

_____

FEBRUARY

EVERY SOBER DAY IS A MIRACLE

Meeting Schedule

Date	Time	Group

EVERY SOBER DAY IS A MIRACLE

DATE: DAYS SOBER:

QUOTE OF THE DAY

I FEEL . . .

HAPPY _____ SAD
ENERGETIC _____ TIRED
CALM _____ ANXIOUS

ANY URGES OR CRAVINGS?
YES   NO

COMMENTS:

EVERY SOBER DAY IS A MIRACLE

DATE: _____   DAYS SOBER: _____

QUOTE OF THE DAY

_____

_____

_____

_____

I FEEL . . .

HAPPY   ⟩▭▭▭▭▭▭⟨   SAD

ENERGETIC ⟩▭▭▭▭▭▭⟨   TIRED

CALM   ⟩▭▭▭▭▭▭⟨   ANXIOUS

ANY URGES OR CRAVINGS?

_____ YES   _____ NO

COMMENTS: _____

EVERY SOBER DAY IS A MIRACLE

DATE: DAYS SOBER:

QUOTE OF THE DAY

I FEEL . . .

HAPPY   SAD
ENERGETIC   TIRED
CALM   ANXIOUS

ANY URGES OR CRAVINGS?
YES   NO

COMMENTS:

EVERY SOBER DAY IS A MIRACLE

DATE: _____   DAYS SOBER: _____

QUOTE OF THE DAY

_____

_____

_____

_____

I FEEL . . .

HAPPY ⊂_____⊃ SAD

ENERGETIC ⊂_____⊃ TIRED

CALM ⊂_____⊃ ANXIOUS

ANY URGES OR CRAVINGS?

YES   NO

COMMENTS: _____

Date:

EVERY SOBER DAY IS A MIRACLE

Goals

MileStones

Why Am I Doing This?

What Are Your Struggles?

What Do You Struggle With The Most?
What Support Do You Need?

_____

_____

_____

What Is One Step You Can Take To Work On Your Struggles?

_____

_____

_____

What Do You Need To Stay Sober?

_____

_____

_____

Prevention

Signs You're Struggling or Becoming Overwhelmed?

_____

_____

_____

_____

Coping Skills To Use:

_____

_____

_____

_____

What Gets You Back On Track?

_____

_____

_____

What Do You Love About Sobriety?

_____

_____

_____

_____

REVIEW

How Has Your Addiction Affected Your Life?

What's The Worst Part About Your Addiction?

What Things Have You Learned From Your Struggles?

REVIEW

What Keeps Drawing You Back Into Your Addiction?

_____

_____

_____

How Have You Sabotaged Your Recovery In The Past?

_____

_____

_____

What Does Your Rock Bottom Look Like?

_____

_____

_____

MARCH

EVERY SOBER DAY IS A MIRACLE

Meeting Schedule

Date	Time	Group

EVERY SOBER DAY IS A MIRACLE

DATE: _____   DAYS SOBER: _____

QUOTE OF THE DAY

_____

_____

_____

_____

I FEEL . . .

HAPPY		SAD
ENERGETIC		TIRED
CALM		ANXIOUS

ANY URGES OR CRAVINGS?

YES _____   NO _____

COMMENTS: _____

EVERY SOBER DAY IS A MIRACLE

DATE: _____   DAYS SOBER: _____

QUOTE OF THE DAY

_____

_____

_____

_____

I FEEL . . .

HAPPY	>============<	SAD
ENERGETIC	>============<	TIRED
CALM	>============<	ANXIOUS

ANY URGES OR CRAVINGS?
_____ YES   _____ NO

COMMENTS: _____

EVERY SOBER DAY IS A MIRACLE

DATE: DAYS SOBER:

QUOTE OF THE DAY

I FEEL . . .

HAPPY		SAD
ENERGETIC		TIRED
CALM		ANXIOUS

ANY URGES OR CRAVINGS?

YES   NO

COMMENTS:

EVERY SOBER DAY IS A MIRACLE

DATE: _____ DAYS SOBER: _____

QUOTE OF THE DAY

_____

_____

_____

_____

I FEEL . . .

HAPPY ⟨_____⟩ SAD

ENERGETIC ⟨_____⟩ TIRED

CALM ⟨_____⟩ ANXIOUS

ANY URGES OR CRAVINGS?

_____ YES _____ NO

COMMENTS: _____

Date:

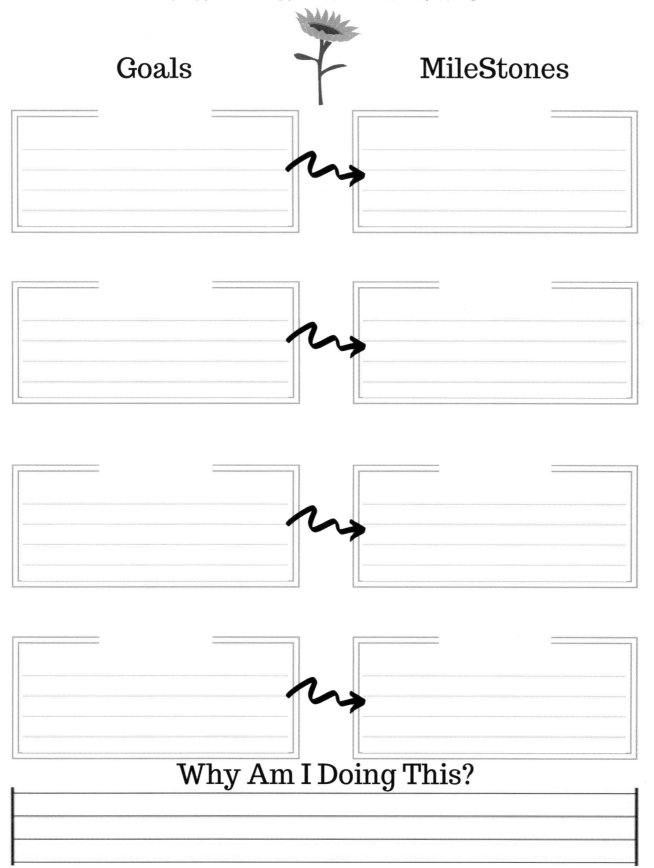

Goals

MileStones

Why Am I Doing This?

What Are Your Struggles?

What Do You Struggle With The Most?
What Support Do You Need?

_____

_____

_____

What Is One Step You Can Take To Work On Your Struggles?

_____

_____

_____

What Do You Need To Stay Sober?

_____

_____

_____

Prevention

Signs You're Struggling or Becoming Overwhelmed?

_____

_____

_____

Coping Skills To Use:

_____

_____

_____

What Gets You Back On Track?

_____

_____

What Do You Love About Sobriety?

_____

_____

_____

REVIEW

How Has Your Addiction Affected Your Life?

_____

_____

_____

What's The Worst Part About Your Addiction?

_____

_____

_____

What Things Have You Learned From Your Struggles?

_____

_____

_____

REVIEW

What Keeps Drawing You Back Into Your Addiction?

_____

_____

_____

How Have You Sabotaged Your Recovery In The Past?

_____

_____

_____

What Does Your Rock Bottom Look Like?

_____

_____

_____

APRIL

EVERY SOBER DAY IS A MIRACLE

Meeting Schedule

Date	Time	Group

EVERY SOBER DAY IS A MIRACLE

DATE: _____ DAYS SOBER: _____

QUOTE OF THE DAY

_____

_____

_____

_____

I FEEL . . .

HAPPY	⟨_____⟩	SAD
ENERGETIC	⟨_____⟩	TIRED
CALM	⟨_____⟩	ANXIOUS

ANY URGES OR CRAVINGS?

YES _____ NO _____

COMMENTS: _____

EVERY SOBER DAY IS A MIRACLE

DATE: _____   DAYS SOBER: _____

QUOTE OF THE DAY

_____

_____

_____

_____

I FEEL . . .

HAPPY		SAD
ENERGETIC		TIRED
CALM		ANXIOUS

ANY URGES OR CRAVINGS?

_____ YES   _____ NO

COMMENTS: _____

DATE: DAYS SOBER:

QUOTE OF THE DAY

I FEEL . . .

HAPPY   SAD

ENERGETIC   TIRED

CALM   ANXIOUS

ANY URGES OR CRAVINGS?

YES   NO

COMMENTS:

DATE: _____ DAYS SOBER: _____

QUOTE OF THE DAY

_____

_____

_____

_____

I FEEL . . .

HAPPY ⟨_____⟩ SAD

ENERGETIC ⟨_____⟩ TIRED

CALM ⟨_____⟩ ANXIOUS

ANY URGES OR CRAVINGS?

_____ YES _____ NO

COMMENTS: _____

Date:

EVERY SOBER DAY IS A MIRACLE

Goals

MileStones

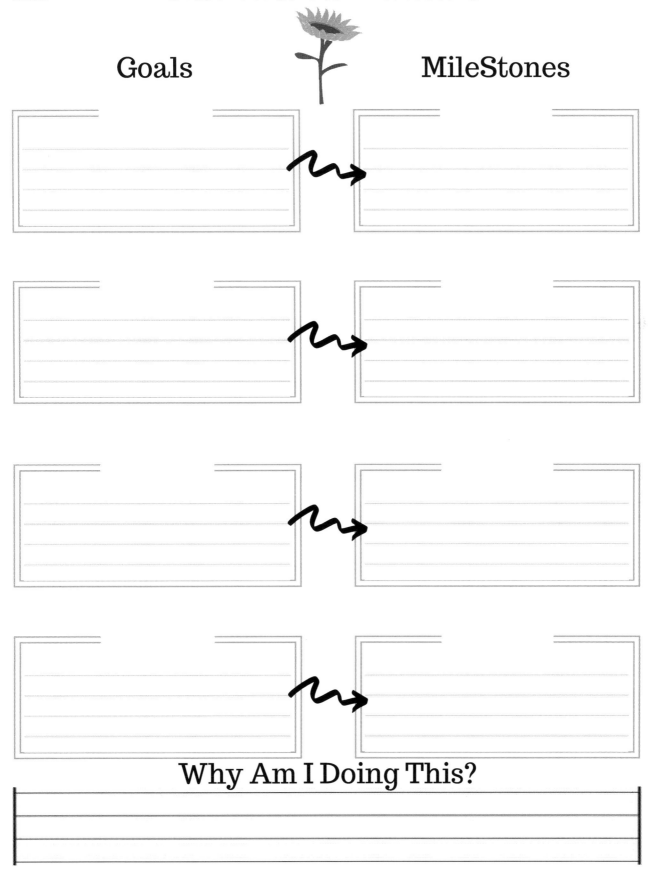

Why Am I Doing This?

What Are Your Struggles?

What Do You Struggle With The Most?
What Support Do You Need?

_____

_____

_____

What Is One Step You Can Take To Work On Your Struggles?

_____

_____

_____

What Do You Need To Stay Sober?

_____

_____

_____

Prevention

Signs You're Struggling or Becoming Overwhelmed?

_____

_____

_____

Coping Skills To Use:

_____

_____

_____

What Gets You Back On Track?

_____

_____

What Do You Love About Sobriety?

_____

_____

_____

REVIEW

How Has Your Addiction Affected Your Life?

_____

_____

_____

_____

What's The Worst Part About Your Addiction?

_____

_____

_____

_____

What Things Have You Learned From Your Struggles?

_____

_____

_____

_____

REVIEW

What Keeps Drawing You Back Into Your Addiction?

How Have You Sabotaged Your Recovery In The Past?

What Does Your Rock Bottom Look Like?

MAY

EVERY SOBER DAY IS A MIRACLE

Meeting Schedule

Date	Time	Group

EVERY SOBER DAY IS A MIRACLE

DATE: DAYS SOBER:

QUOTE OF THE DAY

_____

_____

_____

_____

I FEEL . . .

HAPPY   [   ]   SAD

ENERGETIC   [   ]   TIRED

CALM   [   ]   ANXIOUS

ANY URGES OR CRAVINGS?

YES   NO

COMMENTS:

EVERY SOBER DAY IS A MIRACLE

DATE: _____ DAYS SOBER: _____

QUOTE OF THE DAY

_____

_____

_____

_____

I FEEL . . .

HAPPY	⟩▭⟨	SAD
ENERGETIC	⟩▭⟨	TIRED
CALM	⟩▭⟨	ANXIOUS

ANY URGES OR CRAVINGS?

_____ YES   _____ NO

COMMENTS: _____

EVERY SOBER DAY IS A MIRACLE

DATE: DAYS SOBER:

QUOTE OF THE DAY

_____

_____

_____

I FEEL . . .

HAPPY   [_____]   SAD

ENERGETIC [_____] TIRED

CALM   [_____]   ANXIOUS

ANY URGES OR CRAVINGS?

YES   NO

COMMENTS:

EVERY SOBER DAY IS A MIRACLE

DATE: _____   DAYS SOBER: _____

QUOTE OF THE DAY

_____

_____

_____

_____

I FEEL . . .

HAPPY ◁═══════════════▷ SAD

ENERGETIC ◁═══════════════▷ TIRED

CALM ◁═══════════════▷ ANXIOUS

ANY URGES OR CRAVINGS?

_____ YES   _____ NO

COMMENTS: _____

Date:

EVERY SOBER DAY IS A MIRACLE

Goals

MileStones

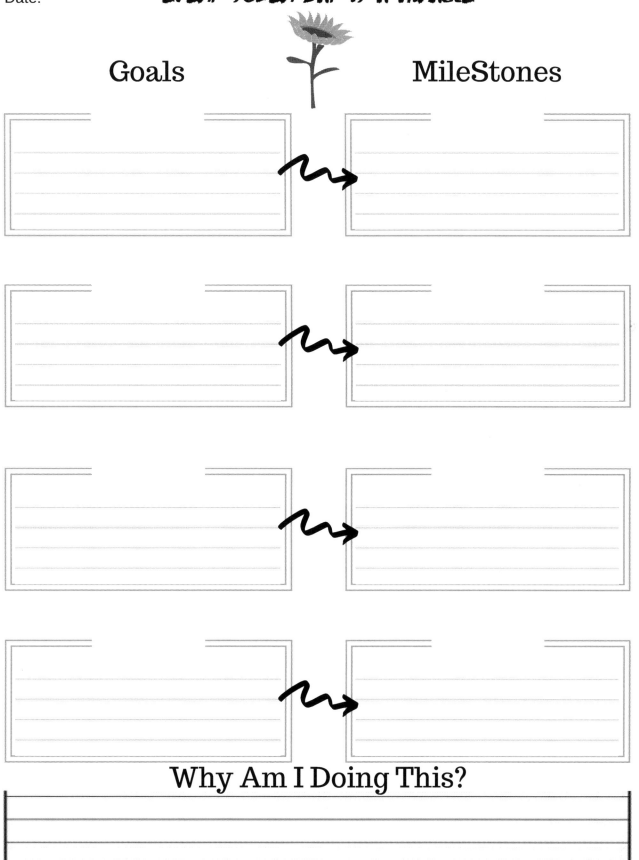

Why Am I Doing This?

What Are Your Struggles?

What Do You Struggle With The Most?
What Support Do You Need?

What Is One Step You Can Take To Work On Your Struggles?

What Do You Need To Stay Sober?

Prevention

Signs You're Struggling or Becoming Overwhelmed?

_____

_____

_____

Coping Skills To Use:

_____

_____

_____

What Gets You Back On Track?

_____

_____

_____

What Do You Love About Sobriety?

_____

_____

_____

REVIEW

How Has Your Addiction Affected Your Life?

What's The Worst Part About Your Addiction?

What Things Have You Learned From Your Struggles?

REVIEW

What Keeps Drawing You Back Into Your Addiction?

How Have You Sabotaged Your Recovery In The Past?

What Does Your Rock Bottom Look Like?

JUNE

EVERY SOBER DAY IS A MIRACLE

Meeting Schedule

Date	Time	Group

EVERY SOBER DAY IS A MIRACLE

DATE: DAYS SOBER:

QUOTE OF THE DAY

I FEEL . . .

HAPPY   SAD

ENERGETIC   TIRED

CALM   ANXIOUS

ANY URGES OR CRAVINGS?
YES   NO

COMMENTS:

EVERY SOBER DAY IS A MIRACLE

DATE: _____   DAYS SOBER: _____

QUOTE OF THE DAY

_____

_____

_____

_____

I FEEL . . .

HAPPY ⟩_____⟨ SAD

ENERGETIC ⟩_____⟨ TIRED

CALM ⟩_____⟨ ANXIOUS

ANY URGES OR CRAVINGS?
_____ YES   _____ NO

COMMENTS: _____

EVERY SOBER DAY IS A MIRACLE

DATE: DAYS SOBER:

QUOTE OF THE DAY

_____

_____

_____

_____

I FEEL . . .

HAPPY	=======================	SAD
ENERGETIC	=======================	TIRED
CALM	=======================	ANXIOUS

ANY URGES OR CRAVINGS?

YES   NO
_____   _____

COMMENTS:

EVERY SOBER DAY IS A MIRACLE

DATE: _____ DAYS SOBER: _____

QUOTE OF THE DAY

_____

_____

_____

_____

I FEEL . . .

HAPPY ⟩_____⟨ SAD

ENERGETIC ⟩_____⟨ TIRED

CALM ⟩_____⟨ ANxIOUS

ANY URGES OR CRAVINGS?
_____ YES _____ NO

COMMENTS: _____

Date:

EVERY SOBER DAY IS A MIRACLE

Goals

MileStones

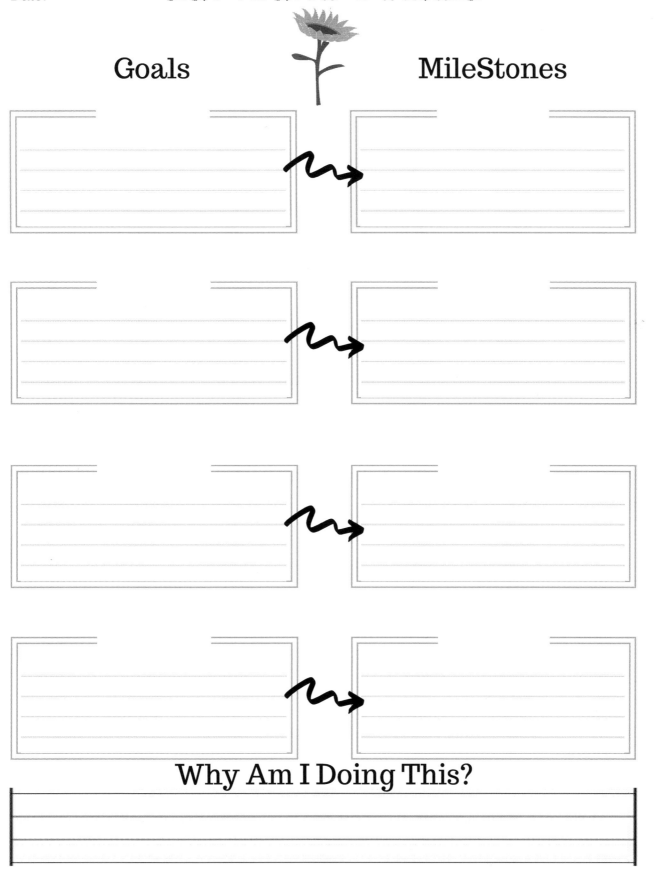

Why Am I Doing This?

What Are Your Struggles?

What Do You Struggle With The Most?
What Support Do You Need?

_____

_____

_____

What Is One Step You Can Take To Work On Your Struggles?

_____

_____

_____

What Do You Need To Stay Sober?

_____

_____

_____

Prevention

Signs You're Struggling or Becoming Overwhelmed?

_____

_____

_____

Coping Skills To Use:

_____

_____

_____

What Gets You Back On Track?

_____

_____

What Do You Love About Sobriety?

_____

_____

_____

REVIEW

How Has Your Addiction Affected Your Life?

_____

_____

_____

What's The Worst Part About Your Addiction?

_____

_____

_____

What Things Have You Learned From Your Struggles?

_____

_____

_____

REVIEW

What Keeps Drawing You Back Into Your Addiction?

_____

_____

_____

How Have You Sabotaged Your Recovery In The Past?

_____

_____

_____

What Does Your Rock Bottom Look Like?

_____

_____

_____

JULY

EVERY SOBER DAY IS A MIRACLE

Meeting Schedule

Date	Time	Group

EVERY SOBER DAY IS A MIRACLE

DATE: DAYS SOBER:

QUOTE OF THE DAY

I FEEL . . .

HAPPY   SAD
ENERGETIC   TIRED
CALM   ANXIOUS

ANY URGES OR CRAVINGS?
YES   NO

COMMENTS:

EVERY SOBER DAY IS A MIRACLE

DATE: _____   DAYS SOBER: _____

QUOTE OF THE DAY

_____

_____

_____

I FEEL . . .

HAPPY _____ SAD

ENERGETIC _____ TIRED

CALM _____ ANXIOUS

ANY URGES OR CRAVINGS?

YES _____   NO _____

COMMENTS: _____

EVERY SOBER DAY IS A MIRACLE

DATE: DAYS SOBER:

QUOTE OF THE DAY

_____

_____

_____

_____

I FEEL . . .

HAPPY   >================<   SAD
ENERGETIC >================<   TIRED
CALM   >================<   ANXIOUS

ANY URGES OR CRAVINGS?
YES   NO

COMMENTS:

EVERY SOBER DAY IS A MIRACLE

DATE: _____   DAYS SOBER: _____

QUOTE OF THE DAY

_____

_____

_____

_____

I FEEL . . .

HAPPY   >————————————<   SAD

ENERGETIC > ————————————<   TIRED

CALM   >————————————<   ANXIOUS

ANY URGES OR CRAVINGS?
_____ YES   _____ NO

COMMENTS: _____

Date:

EVERY SOBER DAY IS A MIRACLE

Goals

MileStones

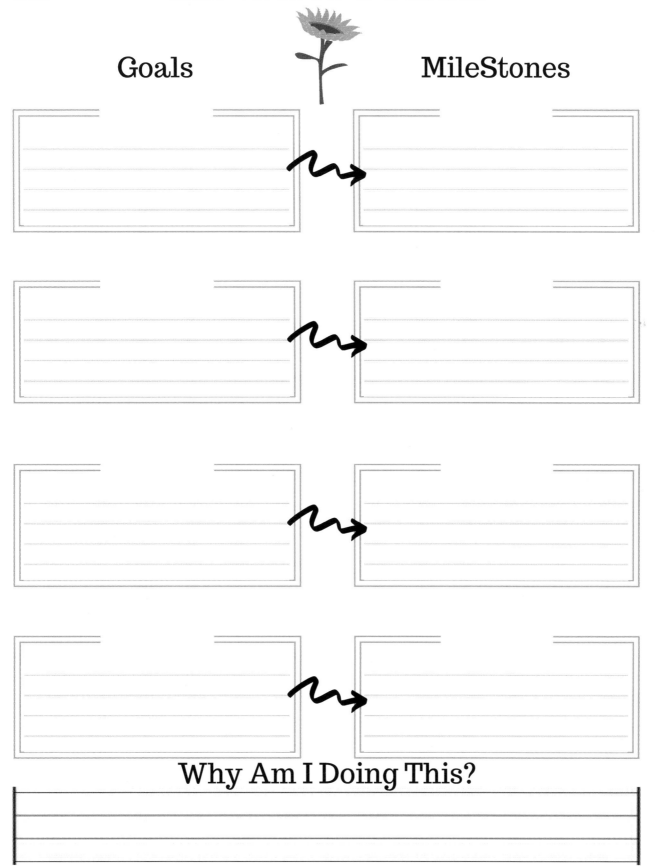

Why Am I Doing This?

What Are Your Struggles?

What Do You Struggle With The Most?
What Support Do You Need?

_____

_____

_____

What Is One Step You Can Take To Work On Your Struggles?

_____

_____

_____

What Do You Need To Stay Sober?

_____

_____

_____

_____

Prevention

Signs You're Struggling or Becoming Overwhelmed?

_____

_____

_____

Coping Skills To Use:

_____

_____

_____

What Gets You Back On Track?

_____

_____

_____

What Do You Love About Sobriety?

_____

_____

_____

REVIEW

How Has Your Addiction Affected Your Life?

_____

_____

_____

_____

What's The Worst Part About Your Addiction?

_____

_____

_____

_____

What Things Have You Learned From Your Struggles?

_____

_____

_____

_____

REVIEW

What Keeps Drawing You Back Into Your Addiction?

_____

_____

_____

How Have You Sabotaged Your Recovery In The Past?

_____

_____

_____

What Does Your Rock Bottom Look Like?

_____

_____

_____

AUGUST

EVERY SOBER DAY IS A MIRACLE

Meeting Schedule

Date	Time	Group

EVERY SOBER DAY IS A MIRACLE

DATE: DAYS SOBER:

QUOTE OF THE DAY

I FEEL . . .

HAPPY   SAD
ENERGETIC   TIRED
CALM   ANXIOUS

ANY URGES OR CRAVINGS?
YES   NO

COMMENTS:

DATE: DAYS SOBER:

QUOTE OF THE DAY

I FEEL . . .

HAPPY		SAD
ENERGETIC		TIRED
CALM		ANXIOUS

ANY URGES OR CRAVINGS?

YES   NO

COMMENTS:

EVERY SOBER DAY IS A MIRACLE

DATE: _____   DAYS SOBER: _____

QUOTE OF THE DAY

_____

_____

_____

_____

I FEEL . . .

HAPPY ⟩————————————⟨ SAD

ENERGETIC ⟩————————————⟨ TIRED

CALM ⟩————————————⟨ ANXIOUS

ANY URGES OR CRAVINGS?

YES _____   NO _____

COMMENTS: _____

EVERY SOBER DAY IS A MIRACLE

DATE: _____   DAYS SOBER: _____

QUOTE OF THE DAY

_____

_____

_____

_____

I FEEL . . .

HAPPY	▭	SAD
ENERGETIC	▭	TIRED
CALM	▭	ANXIOUS

ANY URGES OR CRAVINGS?

____ YES   ____ NO

COMMENTS: _____

Date:

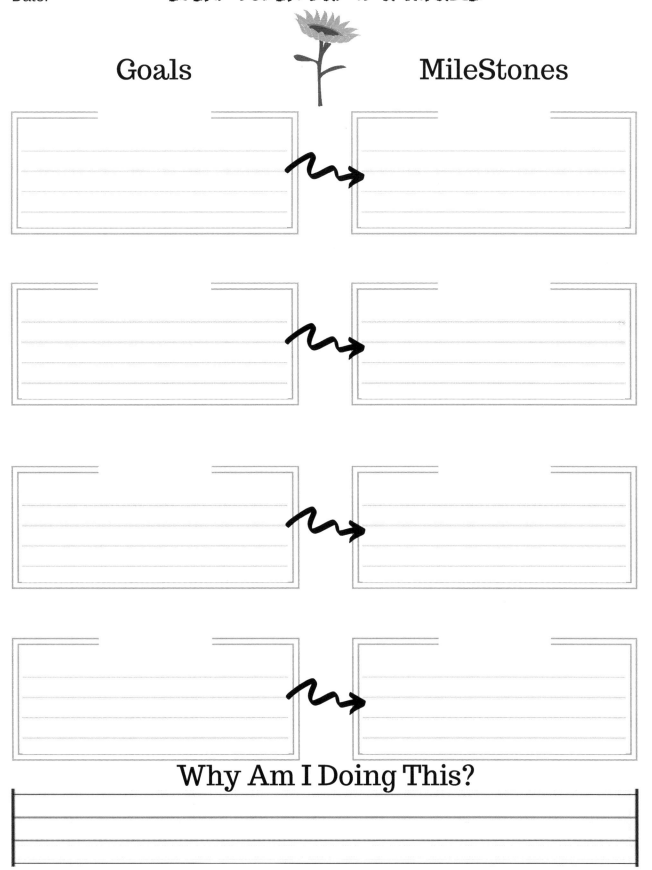

Goals

MileStones

Why Am I Doing This?

What Are Your Struggles?

What Do You Struggle With The Most?
What Support Do You Need?

_____

_____

_____

What Is One Step You Can Take To Work On Your Struggles?

_____

_____

_____

What Do You Need To Stay Sober?

_____

_____

_____

Prevention

Signs You're Struggling or Becoming Overwhelmed?

Coping Skills To Use:

What Gets You Back On Track?

What Do You Love About Sobriety?

REVIEW

How Has Your Addiction Affected Your Life?

What's The Worst Part About Your Addiction?

What Things Have You Learned From Your Struggles?

REVIEW

What Keeps Drawing You Back Into Your Addiction?

_____

_____

_____

How Have You Sabotaged Your Recovery In The Past?

_____

_____

_____

What Does Your Rock Bottom Look Like?

_____

_____

_____

SEPTEMBER

EVERY SOBER DAY IS A MIRACLE

Meeting 🌻 Schedule

Date	Time	Group

DATE: _____   DAYS SOBER: _____

QUOTE OF THE DAY

_____

_____

_____

_____

I FEEL . . .

HAPPY   ⟩_____⟨   SAD

ENERGETIC ⟩_____⟨ TIRED

CALM   ⟩_____⟨ ANXIOUS

ANY URGES OR CRAVINGS?

YES _____   NO _____

COMMENTS: _____

EVERY SOBER DAY IS A MIRACLE

DATE: _____ DAYS SOBER: _____

QUOTE OF THE DAY

_____

_____

_____

_____

I FEEL . . .

HAPPY ⟩_____⟨ SAD

ENERGETIC ⟩_____⟨ TIRED

CALM ⟩_____⟨ ANXIOUS

ANY URGES OR CRAVINGS?
YES _____ NO _____

COMMENTS: _____

EVERY SOBER DAY IS A MIRACLE

DATE: _____   DAYS SOBER: _____

QUOTE OF THE DAY

_____

_____

_____

_____

I FEEL . . .

HAPPY ⟩_____⟨ SAD

ENERGETIC ⟩_____⟨ TIRED

CALM ⟩_____⟨ ANXIOUS

ANY URGES OR CRAVINGS?
YES   NO

COMMENTS:

EVERY SOBER DAY IS A MIRACLE

DATE: _____   DAYS SOBER: _____

QUOTE OF THE DAY

_____

_____

_____

_____

I FEEL . . .

HAPPY   [_____]   SAD

ENERGETIC [_____]   TIRED

CALM   [_____]   ANXIOUS

ANY URGES OR CRAVINGS?

_____ YES   _____ NO

COMMENTS: _____

Date:

EVERY SOBER DAY IS A MIRACLE

Goals

MileStones

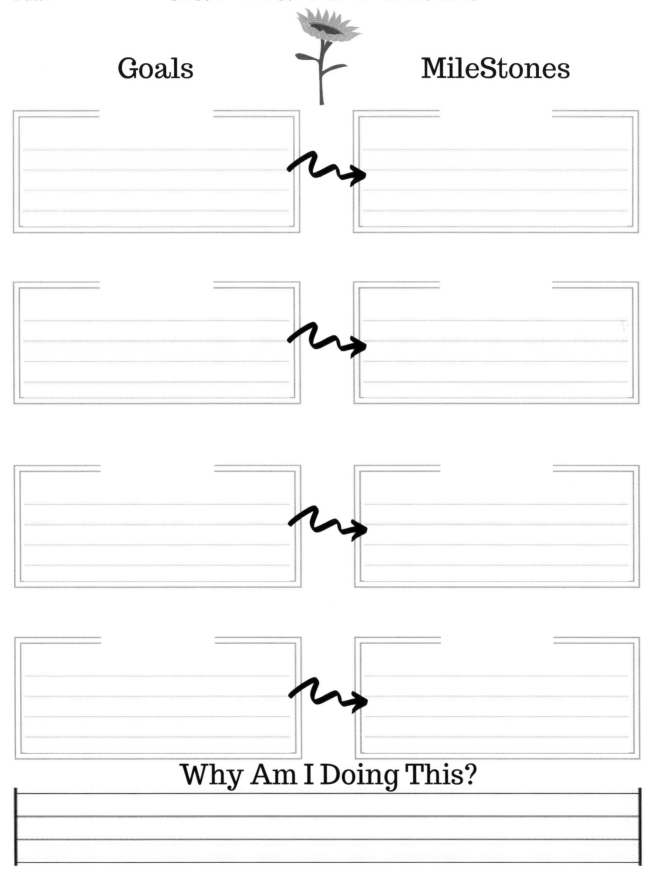

Why Am I Doing This?

What Are Your Struggles?

What Do You Struggle With The Most?
What Support Do You Need?

What Is One Step You Can Take To Work On Your Struggles?

What Do You Need To Stay Sober?

Prevention
Signs You're Struggling or Becoming Overwhelmed?

_____

_____

_____

Coping Skills To Use:

_____

_____

_____

What Gets You Back On Track?

_____

_____

What Do You Love About Sobriety?

_____

_____

_____

REVIEW

How Has Your Addiction Affected Your Life?

What's The Worst Part About Your Addiction?

What Things Have You Learned From Your Struggles?

REVIEW

What Keeps Drawing You Back Into Your Addiction?

_____

_____

_____

_____

How Have You Sabotaged Your Recovery In The Past?

_____

_____

_____

What Does Your Rock Bottom Look Like?

_____

_____

_____

_____

OCTOBER

EVERY SOBER DAY IS A MIRACLE

Meeting Schedule

Date	Time	Group

EVERY SOBER DAY IS A MIRACLE

DATE: DAYS SOBER:

QUOTE OF THE DAY

I FEEL . . .

HAPPY   SAD

ENERGETIC   TIRED

CALM   ANXIOUS

ANY URGES OR CRAVINGS?
YES   NO

COMMENTS:

EVERY SOBER DAY IS A MIRACLE

DATE: _____   DAYS SOBER: _____

QUOTE OF THE DAY

_____

_____

_____

_____

I FEEL . . .

HAPPY ⟨_____⟩ SAD

ENERGETIC ⟨_____⟩ TIRED

CALM ⟨_____⟩ ANXIOUS

ANY URGES OR CRAVINGS?

YES   NO

COMMENTS: _____

EVERY SOBER DAY IS A MIRACLE

DATE: _____   DAYS SOBER: _____

QUOTE OF THE DAY

_____

_____

_____

_____

I FEEL . . .

HAPPY ⟩_____⟨ SAD

ENERGETIC ⟩_____⟨ TIRED

CALM ⟩_____⟨ ANXIOUS

ANY URGES OR CRAVINGS?

YES _____   NO _____

COMMENTS: _____

Date:

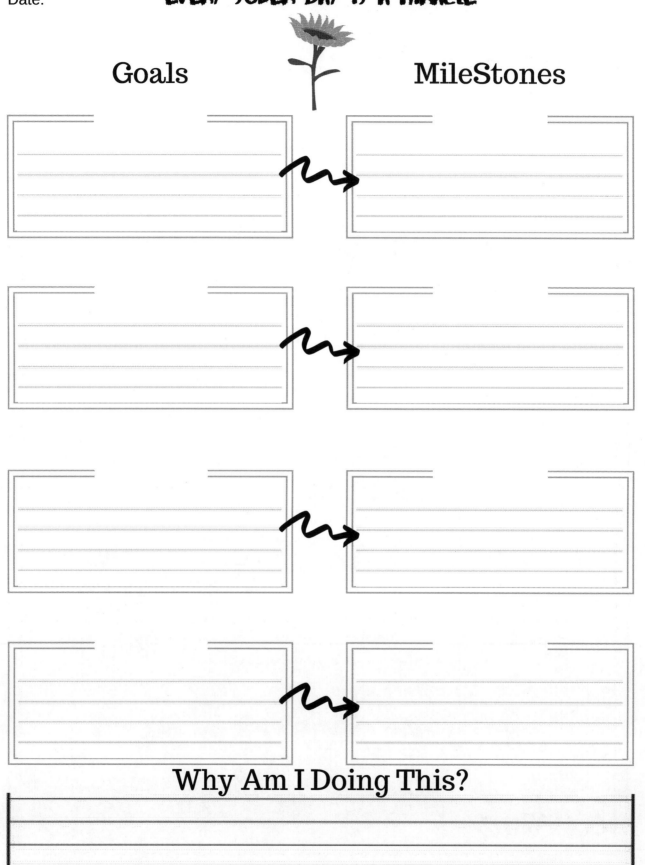

Goals

MileStones

Why Am I Doing This?

What Are Your Struggles?

What Do You Struggle With The Most?
What Support Do You Need?

_____

_____

_____

What Is One Step You Can Take To Work On Your Struggles?

_____

_____

_____

What Do You Need To Stay Sober?

_____

_____

_____

Prevention

Signs You're Struggling or Becoming Overwhelmed?

_____

_____

_____

Coping Skills To Use:

_____

_____

_____

Whats Get You Back On Track?

_____

_____

_____

What Do You Love About Sobriety?

_____

_____

_____

REVIEW

How Has Your Addiction Affected Your Life?

_____

_____

_____

_____

What's The Worst Part About Your Addiction?

_____

_____

_____

_____

What Things Have You Learned From Your Struggles?

_____

_____

_____

_____

REVIEW

What Keeps Drawing You Back Into Your Addiction?

_____

_____

_____

How Have You Sabotaged Your Recovery In The Past?

_____

_____

_____

What Does Your Rock Bottom Look Like?

_____

_____

_____

NOVEMBER
EVERY SOBER DAY IS A MIRACLE

Meeting Schedule

Date	Time	Group

EVERY SOBER DAY IS A MIRACLE

DATE: _____   DAYS SOBER: _____

QUOTE OF THE DAY

_____

_____

_____

_____

I FEEL . . .

HAPPY		SAD
ENERGETIC		TIRED
CALM		ANXIOUS

ANY URGES OR CRAVINGS?

YES _____   NO _____

COMMENTS: _____

EVERY SOBER DAY IS A MIRACLE

DATE: DAYS SOBER:

QUOTE OF THE DAY

I FEEL . . .

HAPPY   SAD
ENERGETIC   TIRED
CALM   ANXIOUS

ANY URGES OR CRAVINGS?
YES   NO

COMMENTS:

EVERY SOBER DAY IS A MIRACLE

DATE: _____   DAYS SOBER: _____

QUOTE OF THE DAY

_____

_____

_____

_____

I FEEL . . .

HAPPY _____ SAD

ENERGETIC _____ TIRED

CALM _____ ANXIOUS

ANY URGES OR CRAVINGS?

_____ YES   _____ NO

COMMENTS: _____

EVERY SOBER DAY IS A MIRACLE

DATE: DAYS SOBER:

QUOTE OF THE DAY

I FEEL . . .

HAPPY _____ SAD

ENERGETIC _____ TIRED

CALM _____ ANXIOUS

ANY URGES OR CRAVINGS?

YES   NO

COMMENTS:

Date:

EVERY SOBER DAY IS A MIRACLE

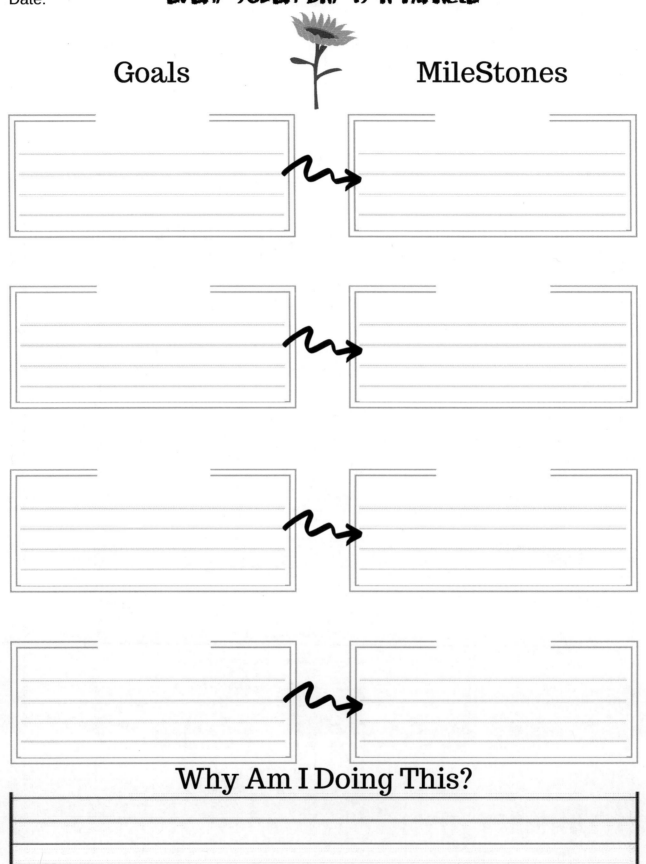

Goals

MileStones

Why Am I Doing This?

What Are Your Struggles?

What Do You Struggle With The Most?
What Support Do You Need?

_____

_____

_____

_____

What Is One Step You Can Take To Work On Your Struggles?

_____

_____

_____

_____

What Do You Need To Stay Sober?

_____

_____

_____

_____

Prevention

Signs You're Struggling or Becoming Overwhelmed?

Coping Skills To Use:

What Gets You Back On Track?

What Do You Love About Sobriety?

REVIEW

How Has Your Addiction Affected Your Life?

_____

_____

_____

_____

What's The Worst Part About Your Addiction?

_____

_____

_____

_____

What Things Have You Learned From Your Struggles?

_____

_____

_____

_____

REVIEW

What Keeps Drawing You Back Into Your Addiction?

_____

_____

_____

_____

How Have You Sabotaged Your Recovery In The Past?

_____

_____

_____

_____

What Does Your Rock Bottom Look Like?

_____

_____

_____

_____

DECEMBER
EVERY SOBER DAY IS A MIRACLE

Meeting Schedule

Date	Time	Group

EVERY SOBER DAY IS A MIRACLE

DATE: _____   DAYS SOBER: _____

QUOTE OF THE DAY

_____

_____

_____

_____

I FEEL . . .

HAPPY		SAD
ENERGETIC		TIRED
CALM		ANxIOUS

ANY URGES OR CRAVINGS?

_____ YES   _____ NO

COMMENTS: _____

EVERY SOBER DAY IS A MIRACLE

DATE: DAYS SOBER:

QUOTE OF THE DAY

I FEEL . . .

HAPPY   SAD

ENERGETIC   TIRED

CALM   ANXIOUS

ANY URGES OR CRAVINGS?

YES   NO

COMMENTS:

EVERY SOBER DAY IS A MIRACLE

DATE: _____   DAYS SOBER: _____

QUOTE OF THE DAY

_____

_____

_____

_____

I FEEL . . .

HAPPY   ⟨_____⟩   SAD

ENERGETIC ⟨_____⟩ TIRED

CALM   ⟨_____⟩   ANXIOUS

ANY URGES OR CRAVINGS?

_____ YES   _____ NO

COMMENTS: _____

EVERY SOBER DAY IS A MIRACLE

DATE: _____ DAYS SOBER: _____

QUOTE OF THE DAY

_____

_____

_____

I FEEL . . .

HAPPY ⟩_____⟨ SAD

ENERGETIC ⟩_____⟨ TIRED

CALM ⟩_____⟨ ANXIOUS

ANY URGES OR CRAVINGS?

YES _____ NO _____

COMMENTS: _____

Date:

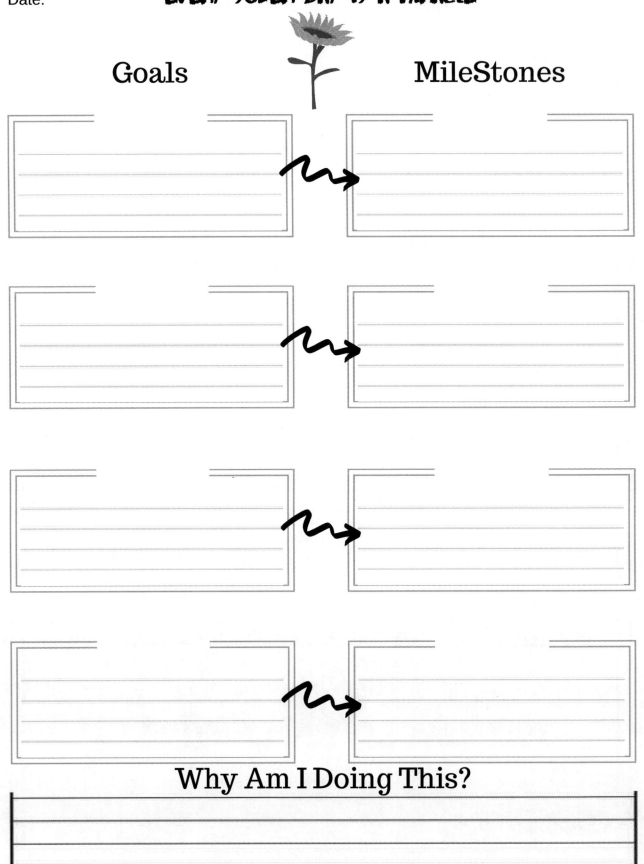

Goals

MileStones

Why Am I Doing This?

What Are Your Struggles?

What Do You Struggle With The Most?
What Support Do You Need?

_____

_____

_____

What Is One Step You Can Take To Work On Your Struggles?

_____

_____

_____

What Do You Need To Stay Sober?

_____

_____

_____

Prevention

Signs You're Struggling or Becoming Overwhelmed?

_____

_____

_____

Coping Skills To Use:

_____

_____

_____

Whats Get You Back On Track?

_____

_____

_____

What Do You Love About Sobriety?

_____

_____

_____

REVIEW

How Has Your Addiction Affected Your Life?

_____

_____

_____

What's The Worst Part About Your Addiction?

_____

_____

_____

What Things Have You Learned From Your Struggles?

_____

_____

_____

REVIEW

What Keeps Drawing You Back Into Your Addiction?

_____

_____

_____

How Have You Sabotaged Your Recovery In The Past?

_____

_____

_____

What Does Your Rock Bottom Look Like?

_____

_____

_____

NOTES

DRAW MY LIFE
BEFORE SOBRIETY

Date:

wHAT HAVE YOU ACCOMPLISHED IN 3 MONTHS?

HOW DO YOU FEEL ABOUT YOUR ACCOMPLISHMENTS?

DRAW MY LIFE
AFTER 3 MONTHS SOBRIETY

I'M THANKFUL
FOR

NOTES

Date:

wHAT HAVE YOU ACCOMPLISHED IN 6 MONTHS?

HOW DO YOU FEEL ABOUT YOUR ACCOMPLISHMENTS?

DRAW MY LIFE
AFTER 6MONTHS SOBRIETY

I'M THANKFUL
FOR

NOTES

Date:

wHAT HAVE YOU ACCOMPLISHED IN 9 MONTHS?

HOW DO YOU FEEL ABOUT YOUR ACCOMPLISHMENTS?

DRAW MY LIFE
AFTER 9MONTHS SOBRIETY

I'M THANKFUL FOR

NOTES

Date:

wHAT HAVE YOU ACCOMPLISHED IN 12 MONTHS?

HOW DO YOU FEEL ABOUT YOUR ACCOMPLISHMENTS?

DRAW MY LIFE
1YR AGO SOBRIETY

DRAW MY LIFE
AFTER 12MONTHS SOBRIETY

I'M THANKFUL
FOR

NOTES

NOTES

NOTES

NOTES

NOTES

NOTES

NOTES

NOTES

NOTES

NOTES

Made in the USA
Las Vegas, NV
21 April 2022